# mylar

# mylar

Eric Wertheimer

BlazeVOX [books]
Buffalo, NY

*publisher of weird little books*

# BlazeVOX [ books ]

blazevox.org

2   4   6   8   0   9   7   5   3   1

BlazeVOX

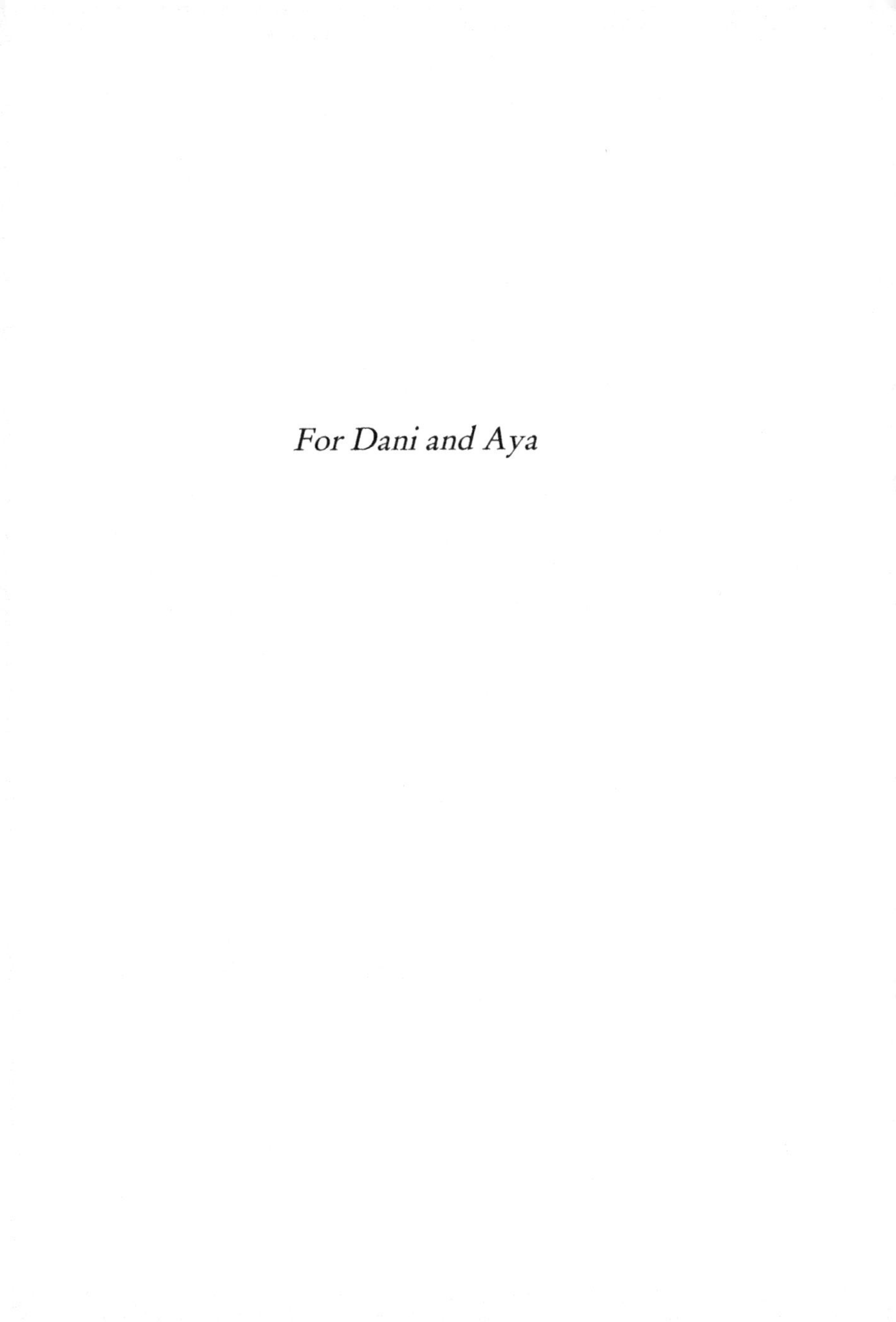

*For Dani and Aya*

# Table of Contents

# mylar

# 1. Preparatory Meditations

The Kites

In West's painting "Benjamin Franklin Drawing Electricity

from the Sky"

Franklin's friends appear as unwinged angels, an effluence

of a storm.

But after a moment, they are what they are--only slaves

hard at work on modernity's indispensable rhombus, the

kite.


Their job is to anchor the line, to see that it

Points to the west and beyond,  keeping the key

--a double O-o—w, blacker even than the sky

they ignore—aloft for Ben's righteous fist.


They subject the great man to a minor

charge while others labor on more modern

generators and conductors, round fire,

in a calibrated genius of serene uncharacteristic disregard.


Franklin the hero is too handsome here.

And the poor little "angels of reason" are ugly in calculated

contrast, puggishly balding, too determined around the

eyes,

as they administer aid from the sub-regions of big cogito.


In Ben's uncelestially linked hand, there is a scrolled cloth

or paper, a careless gesture to the earth,

a connecting figure between the new

dialogues, above and below, self-annihilating strike.


No one is wet in Pennsylvania.  They are blown by an

eastern wind.

They reveal nothing in their tasteful resistance to invisible

forces.

Is the head--the cerebrum as it appears beneath hair, bone,

and cloud--

tantamount to the mind?  Is the center of this scene a capital

monster, with blind contraptions and sparks careening in

oil?


Another kite soars like a sea-phantom in the blackest part

of the sky,

above his mind.  And the small fiends

who minister his knuckled frequency do not know to fear

its omen.  Ben himself seems to launch this second kite

from the dark side of his authority, the leeward position of

change.


There is not enough of the kite here to trust the data,

which makes for a kind of distant satire.

It is enough to know that the line itself is important;

it is the kite, producing

the kite.

Think of the incurious spindles, the slack that must have

sped

out line upon line, Benjamin doubled,

in the agonized rolls of worry and

in the cool fastness of sight.


As if to say:

These sheets, all made gray, to the wind.

## Wellstone



I thought your shoes were birds.

I felt a foot keeping them in place

above the floor, but pinioned to a

beat, very cold.  That meant sit still

to me, that I cannot stake a bridge

while air chokes in the manmade heat.


Which was a parent, a flight that fear ended,

a drive instead to what was now my and

your familiar.  I thought your shoes were

birds.  Fans blew water through huge doors

and wheels did not hinder the destruction

of the Inca nor the Maya.  Wheels were

shoes by another name.


At that point in the season we began to

look ahead, knowing that to go there

is only to assume the travel and lay by

the work.  What each day brings is

the making old of recent news,

those incapable of updating.

The odor of rubber and waiting.


What really frightens me about those planes

is not the possibility of murder they affirm,

but the scrim of corporate dying

they prove.  A smooth overbright

end, *molten aluminum sounds*

*like it,* the looming in *um.*

Yes, dying is a fall within the mouth.

Partnership like fire, death without death.


Do you recall, Alisa,

when I saw you at the assembly,

the very moment winged eyes set on you?

There was *nothing* above us,

in the sky in 1973.

I thought your shoes were birds.

Spielberg

Margaret: "Money is,

In the long pull of time, still money."

To which he:"No it's not,

that is why we're here."


Bottom line of money's

sortilege, Midas would argue with jewelers

(whose jingle is not to

be trusted by those who sought


a wounding) he'd fall

and say "value" is what can

be seen with thine eyes, or had he known, what parts

of Christ we can jar into beauty and

count languidly at card tables.

In the newer regions of sorrow.

some kings can turn trains around

with the twist of a finger and say to the rest,


go hide.  Who was Midas then?

And what would the gentiles in

Tim's gang have to say to history's best sleight,

the touchstone of heaps and


transformations, around which the wind falls?

" Money can't be seen, that is why we are here."

And what of money, in analytic truth?

Could anyone avoid its probing eyes and liquid calm,


a burned femur buried safe

in an old velvet bag;

or resist in all sincerity

the tragic veil of Saint Veronica?

Three Buts

But I just smell the sign of her relatives

are building up for pain and suffering to get

a killing.


But this day has a comic sky,

the sky Stevens thought of

when he used the word comic,

so unsure of its own meaning

that it makes frantic its own natural

discovery. Helen Keller

might decode what is there,

the promiscuity above:

Offset blue against

carbon, putting one cloud

too low, like a mountain rising suddenly

in a doorframe.

Or trying clouds as contrails,

a run of lines that are not

axiomatic, but accidents plain and simple,

no destinations or letters or crude animals.

Why should they originate there

and then plotz all over the horizon?

Back to the fishtank light,

the sun blows cold, sets fire to the mud

and wet gravel.

The sun burns the world.


But radiation washed the stone age

too, rocketing the earth, for maiden

tocsins and tabulation's

bones were born then.

Thus enlarging

dawn redwood and

iridium line, the marrow

of silicon depletes to illness

and thoughtless switching.

Suffering in the snow of Gaul,

mystified brave by

undeveloped comprehension

thick face and uncertain aches--

he rued the magnet of time and

clicked rhythms to the great

transponding diocese of magic.

He did not speak in the shrouded

triplicate of the religious, he

barreled out of foreboding,

promoting the home-based

business to be, that would be ours.

It was time to hang up.

This ungrasped home

found no fractal horn.

My daughter knows,

in spite of the answer, it was no one

who called this evening.

## What Occurs Outside of a Box

The mountains are idle like

wrenches in a box. Your harrowing chants

and nouns have a suspect nose;

they are adjectives hiding within a name

walking to the lens, shifting blame;

organizations as opposed to networks.

Thoreau moped the south shore,

sifting the empty waves for signs of

sovereign Margaret.

Luke appeared in the patterned glass,

prismatic and innocently broken.

We sent him away.

The search for a reason to be angry,

turned on the day again, and then more;

his body was bulleted and fabulous.

and these, over here,

are the shoes he died in.

# Preparatory Meditations

"My heart shall be thy Chrystall looking glass shewing thy lilies face most cleare in mee in shape and beauty that doth brightly flash…"
—Edward Taylor


They aren't guilty, really, the ones on television news. The victims are just you--child slaves, murder survivors, grieving, ripped off, excited witnesses. But they show up so ready so subjunctive so full of other syntax to present their cases. They snipe their cameos, they know their scripts, they only have stories they think must be known, when they ought to know how disproportionate their suffering is in the world they fill. Maybe they should be excused; they are insolvent. For who can understand when all you see is yourself in some crazed fire, the way you are meant to be, meant by the facts of what we experience. Here, before those.

# 2. Mylar

Mylar



There are four balloons

in my house.  I live in the house

with four balloons, two get wells


and one happy birthday and one

you did it.  One lives in the back of a

closet at the end of a hollow plastic stick.


It only moves when I find it.  But it

never leaves.  The other three migrate

along the ceiling, riding


registered air,  a smooth pasture

not unmoved as the seasons require—

send them shining all around here.

They progress from room to room and

fool me with their corporation.

But they are my ghosts.


But they surprise me with their bridal entries

and their mocking murmurs,

their bright entrapment, their


lively ventures in freedom.

The spirit of Mickey Mouse inhabits them

and with their demise, one by one,


I plan to inspire him and then

wonder who am I when I speak.

I am amazed they do not die now, that they

are stable.  Unlike the living,

they never lose it.  When people are

here, I don't notice them.

Solitaire

This menu of starts

Excessive deals and

Draws.  The nervous

Retrominge that selects

Undo.  An ace should go

There, followed soon

By whatever you can

Pull.  And drag.

If you do it as fast as

You can, there is small

Comfort, in the length

Of losses.  They all come

In threes, but every fraction

Draws its own probable

Sum, the end game, sometimes

Visible from the first

Turning over.  You lose

Without a move.  Your

Love is a boat with two

Hulls.  The whacky

Unshuffle that greets

A win, precedes the

Stacking of the deck.

Where is losing?

In soft land

Predicated on hardcut

Logic, a marketing

Rather than a gaming.

Or the same kind of

Luck, four hundred years old,

Done with hand and face.

Or the hardware, the weary

Grip that

Grasps you back, that chains

You radial to a breasted

Ease? No more questions

No more backwards

thinking.

Time for a free cell.

The Murderer's Clothes

I opened the drier and
pulled out a pair of khakis and a t-shirt.
They were enormous.  These
must be some sort of costume, some play
clothes for my daughters.  They
were size 60 waist and 30 inseam,
the white shirt a xxx-large.

> [I had to leave then.
> There was no way
> else, else a reduction
> in breathing.  So here
> I am eleven stories
> up on the folks behind
> me.  Below,
> bagels and discolored
> squares.  Waiting for my
> feet.  They are so damned angry.
> Last ones on.  Save the shaking
> finger at them.]

As Milagros began to iron,
I remembered--
they belong to the double murderer

she is defending.  The one
with hair more beautiful
even than hers.

The Receiver



Watching the movie Bounce

about an executive played by Affleck

who lucks out  of a doomed flight and falls

in love with the dead substitute's


lovely wife, Gwyneth, I fall into sleep.

Wake up an hour later at the roll

of the credits and realize my wife

is not home.  This was not


the video I had intended to rent,

but Bounce was in the box designated

O Brother Where Art Thou?

The phone rings and I cannot find


the receiver.  I worry that it is

my wife.  The VCR uncurls

the black tape within,

slobbers universal disappointment,

sticks the tongue of Bounce


out into the dark rewinding room.

The Interruption



She comes home in

a signified portion of

night, when sleep

has worn off for the first time

and the second part of

its closing sets in. For him it is

a moment of preeminent

interruption, and a dire worry

about invasion and loss.

The result is a pulling of what may

never come home again,

a shift away from light,

a salvation in the attended body.


He knows he will dream this again

in the second half of his night,

repeating again and again,

"mediawhoresonline, mediawhoresonline,"

turning this address over the unconscious palate

like a bad meal set against the churn of sleep.


But the interruption is never

fatal.  And she dials into bed

so tired and blue that the myth of

disruption never really takes hold

in the misdirections of his mind.


He dreams it all in the second half,

despite this.  The dream says to him,

"Love is an interruption."

# 3. Catalepsis

# The World

"They took my skull and broke it

just east of my eyes,

cut an equator over my head

from ear to ear, then

swung half of me forward

exposing the frontal cortex.

They lifted my brain

and followed the optic nerve

to the pituitary gland and

removed the tumor.

I was unlucky.  They got rid of the

thing, but damaged the pituitary

while leaving traces of it for fear of

crippling me permanently.  Which

they did anyway, and now I am

fat around the middle.

But here's the fascinating thing.

They told me that it was a kind of

homunculus, an undeveloped mass

of cells, a lost brother,

which found its safest home

in my head from the moment of my

own successful individuation.

My tumor, which has left me

naturally immature, is my twin.

And you were my brother too,

both before my maturity, and now

after it."

# The Clone's Ontology



world within, liver heart and spleen topside,

a philosopher's object,  Mobius aloud.


when squalid reversions of cartilage moan it is

living, being uncleeted and chaotic.


a simple wound, an injection unpunctured, a secret.

defying measurement by two roots,


inverted by rogue figures, torqued left into

the unforecast, the ocean repose beyond.


a kidney, some radar thus,

conjugated before the pretense of selfsameness.

pain was astray, unheard of, a palimpsest in lymph

an impersonal carnage,  violent defect.


in truth the prolapse of a ghost,  cloaking

in viscera,  pastoral resettlement,  this


final correction of tragic prominence.

chickens are blue, dolphins teal,


all eat at the dock of need--

bodies that mack in passive remark.


and last, my heart,  zero object of all their neglect,

pulses even so in turbulent chords.


*Currents around the scratch and slip*

*of my body, sound like words and*

*the excess of scars.*

*Within me you incarnate things.*

Shipbreaking

Geronimo occupied the caves whose steep entry

Needs visitors forget the ground, to angle safely in a

Level shadow.  All along the half-rung rise, prows of old

Film make stops of the air--make the

Past speak like a movie will do in the tracks beneath; and

people

Just walk by, glibly focused on

Blood sugar and melanoma,

Feeling their hips answer.


They do not suppose that

Ships are broken far from the

Ocean, from Bangladesh and its

Tiger-patterned strand.  At its southern reach,

Like the lost curl of a continent, canyon bows hide

Old mining cars stranded halfway up

Looking for their expected chutes, leaving a bilge

Of visored salutes and petitions, above and below

In tourist breakwaters.


The ship leads back northerly out to the cold needle's

Shadow and then divides, bending exactly to

The south again, and east.  The Apaches

Lost the cavalry in galley caves,

Even when the light of day illumined

Them like half moons on Peralta's deck.

Something cracked the ridge in that way, and

The world leaked and was confused

And large knowing birds

Came to rescue its unnerving nestedness.


Even here, where the waves seem to rise

All the way up into darkness, it is possible

Still to see a way home, or at least

The long promise that is your car,

Avast in some cistern cup of morning.

You can see this against the floor of middle

Shoals, which would break you and make

You slide infernal to Mexico,

From the bleeding hold of the earth.

Ingest



The watch started when the rabbit fell,

the carcass a sign along human wash.


Mature coat cloud, smooth near

the shoulder, and tufted near the leg; its killer


put a stamp upon a haunch, slaughtered

for sudden delectation, an edict in camouflage.


The over-biting authenticity of diastema,

minutely cleft symbol of rabbit mouth;


a face disappearing into dirt

as even sharper predators

had excised a clean bit of its desiccation.

[This narrow confusion of guilt and ownership,


a parchment in burial denied.

Parsed into the very hills,


note how possessives are punctuated

the impersonal pronoun not requiring the hanging


comma to signify property.

A suggested life is elided, or smothered, by the attraction


of a small yet versatile talon.]

Its ears ran parallel to its body—a fussy presence.


Wells of disproportionate auricles, flanged like sage,

set upward in pointless hare detection

at the moment of its failing gravity and consequent

squelching.  He heard not even the stone-flies who


answer a congregational demand for landing noise.

Beware the carcass in your haste to return from the

mountain.


Step around it, the watch winds of sloping earth,

for the sun greatens in vulgar openness.


It claims the liberty of symbols

—the (Easter) cross of boulders, warnings against arson


and trespass, against pollution and apostrophe.  Beneath

the early trees and grass of knives,


four green birds go to heaven.

Catalepsis

Songs stopped in progressive

soft retreat, quieter and

then gone, a question in memory of itself


never sure who was doing the stopping

or if it was self-willed,

if a song can be a self or have will.


Some withered after ripeness

fell to the ground of an orchard

left only a little earlier,


farewell the taper of youth

and unfortunate souls who

could not find the time.

Or someone took them away,

deciding their stay in the world

without short songs is enough



for systolic falling.  It resolves to a

style--sorrow in tune, a nostalgia

without specters, or a mirage in water,



repetition without echo.

He realizes that.

To end now is to carry on



and murder Freud where he lives,

to make the lonely familiar

(like what's-his-name



across the alley, with the gun

and the fluttering brain).

Or to stop is to die,


as beginning was to die,

to be cosmic and portentous,

to say "so long" while lungs and


heart bellow on.

(He grew up into theory,

wondered who was fading.)


Songs bulge in

their jukebox terrarium,

and they sound alive there,


youth's mildew on the brow of generation.

Today they exhaust with age

or bind a wound with terse enclosure

as if that world is the diastolic place of

its origin and there is no pity, no possibility

in suspension and seizure, for any other.

## Talking at the Movies

Somewhere in here, I was born.

End your solemn chase, languid

finger near the burden of a thorn.


Ring one:  too long buried

to be of much use, a loop run

by a husband's banded desire.


Unable to grip the final rung of

uncountable stairs.

A farmer's daughter loves you


more than discretely.

By contrast, he is thin enough

to resent what is alert about you;

maybe he is no longer hungry,

but troubled and eager to release from capture

this night's protracted shadow.


Stay, refrain from saying what to do.

Or keen false stanzas of muted fugues;

I'm checking my watch to count the rings


jumped out of sync by exalted tongues.

You've been told--

I've been told by the tide of breath--


the smart set already know this feature.

A hushing delivers you to the waves.

You are unaware of the rising eyes,

the cuts out of frame, out of watch,

the quiet wintering of thorn and wood.

See there, it's you too,



there's some thing in you.

Disambiguation

City of plague.

From afar

the imprint

of a thumb

upon a field

above earth,

by a gulf.

The wave

made into a hand

then inflamed finger

with its

fine ranks

and broken channels

identity beneath a name

pinwheel files.

The white guilt

wrote

on black glass

an arrow north

toward the window.

Its pressurey havoc

a wink

and go ahead

up go fly,

on the ground

there is wind

in the water.

# 4. Dots

Hard to Find

In the observation room

where Aya talks without a voice,

we are together, but separate, in a


movie with a character

returning from the dead (or visited

by customized archangels)


acknowledging contact

or any evidence he is not immersed permanently

in a cruel illusion.  Only today


this falsity is the ruse of convinced

surveillance, intending safety and education--

not jackdaws who ripple the horizon in the name

of something after.  Because I attend this mirrored glass,

searching into the court light of the room,
and alienate by setting eyes on her body itself


an uneven trust--step out number three,

look away five, what do you see in this separation?
I suppose I will return and love that distant


face even more. I think I see her looking through

the impassible mirror, recognizing a profile in the

unlit room I occupy alone.  And in so doing, I fall,


like blinds down a sudden window,
from a very tall chair.

## Of Ordinary Time



Startled by its effective agony, the heat

shivers, exhausted and unamazed

by the alchemy it was struck to repeat, again

a dull cough on a cold night;

two tons to this side insufficient,

an hydraulic push of breath, the heat half,

or a signal that the thing is breaking,

so much space to be responsible for,

you can feel its vented back break each

time the mercury tips out of merciful

favor, and sends it to work, transferring burn to burn,

spinning disaster; call repair

wish the contacts are unruined

by vapor and crystals, trust the labor of its

progressive failure does not find its register

in the new lungs of children

(silver berry bark, lily pollen, gum media).

The bleached night stays the same despite

engines thrown at its secret virus of sorrow,

its uncaring welcome into what it truly is,

white light thrown over to darkness, clear

of the thing that makes it fire by day.

Prosthetic Sirens

You should know what it needs:

a life of careful attention and

miserable rotten luck.

That safe frame has so much potential, one thinks,

all seized into speech that doesn't complete itself,

carrying out, glaring and remote--

a twenty one gun salute

in wide Arabia.

What else does it want?

Bodyrock stumbles.  Purulent weeping.

Early summer clouds.

Plurality itself.

A blowing shadow on cinderblock.

The dance of little girls

And the crest of panic.

A drop of blue rain in

an old movie.

This place.

## Annealing



Where we live, we live in cars
Last summer fetch of wind
Dust storm at the mirror of stars—

And evening, when effects come back
Without the hue of identity--
Aya and the blowy

Ground in dissolving layer air.
At the center of a cube, subdivided by one—
Left only a new sort of dawn

Sere and blasted on auto-glass.
It descended in soothing upheaval
Desert bones blown to scuff

And their horizons finally entered,
The re-sorting of test bombs
From flats the uplands interrupted

Resume their fission in hot valleys.
It distributes saving pressure near us,
And passes the un-breathable wave

Because we warrant annealing,
And promise this (her fingers
Like a starting wind on my knees) .

Television



The girls call it a ride, the automatically scrolling

billboard at the mall.  They

place their hands on its Plexiglas window

waiting the turn of word and image, cheering

the upward departure of pizza, stiletto, jade ring.

Their mother asks impatiently:

Why is everything always *from* somewhere?

New tongues feel inside the float

of meaning, and heel to worship

as though offering a slim dragon their love.

Who, in burning, declines their rich hands. Or,

sensing a beautiful machine making

here there, and then "there" so close,

they let slide mystery in a palisade of illusion.

They are transported without moving.

Television.  Where does it take them, flyers? The answer

is theirs, in the unearned colors of the wingfallen.

It puts them where they go, riding, with

hot fingertips and feathery eyes and

legions feet, at the violet edge of fury.

Trench

He imagined an April of words.

She spoke in measured

falls, heard the circus of birds in the

last hours of night,

and noticed only yesterday that garbage trucks

are the color green, all of them.


He visited convenience

stores to play Scratchers.

Garden Grove

was Moon Valley again.

He drifted into a season of luck.


He advertised miniature satin hands.

A raven arced violet beneath him,

larger than a crow.

"Whose air do we ride

in the incomparable moments of Olympus?"


"Not true, more pain in a pop song than

all of Cambodia; and the fan palms

are phony accessories,

unfit to broom the alkaline skies of Phoenix."

"We can't decide we can't decide."


Listen carefully:

Our words are vestiges

of Greek and Roman tongues,

so rachitic and unsafe

I want to speak in some other way

--no more tressled ologies or planked Saxonisms.


I want to say something to my

dear children and loving wife

in the untensed space of morning.


Here in this late day,

obsolete and found, April.

Dots

*For Elsa Silva, who died January 5th, 2002*


This is all that's left of it, the day she stopped loving

him, a chronic peace in blue morning.


Even the desert sky cleaning Boston's air (with Lowell

money),

and stone arches turning to real mountains, they stay here.


A text made vision itself, like a stone nearness, in full view,

kindness without darkening eyes, waiting to close.


The altar of missals and the cross-sectioned

rhizomes of transacted groves, runway benedictions

through

unpiloted windows, these too fall, patiently, a click machine

of contrasting dots.  What no one ever wanted has made

wanted


a fugitive claim, a frantic series of beautiful grievances,

ideas about what to render when wanting is answered.


Whatever escape pushed through and proclaimed,

the ages have already granted one another.  They who saw

Fidel


in the deep night above Fort Avarice, see only her.  The

smell of infraction on a sweater

like a pointer running from arm to hand, a


lone white rose near blooming shadows on the floor.  The

sky then

was like whey, and nothing had separated in any discernible

mode of old or new,  just texture and the fiction of what

you could see.

Run orthogonal.  Here, goodbye is easy to say.  Water

spoke in a blue hose,


and a shallow step down, and a burning question,

and the late bills, past Xavier's central dome.


It is two months later and Pluto finds a home.

Paralex



I meant to spell "safe" but could only

find the letters for "stove."

An irresistible alphabet

tips your eyes to heart-filled expanse,

as with light at the reaches of air.

Its splendor is in replacement,

held to a background like constellations

of shifting heroes who wheel and return.


They spell you near, only to repel your understanding,

even as they represent the lengthening of the

world.  Sometimes, I'd rather not spell it out, so that

the ends of that world will not become more

distant, the closer you move to this understanding.

I'd like to find the letters for "love,"

though I need to demonstrate how the silent "e"

makes the vowel before the consonant

long and easy-sounding.  But those

letters happen not to be there.  And

the rule I've been tutoring tonight

does not apply in this rare case.


Other cases like love:  "have," "live," and "give."

How do these words arrange on the white metal?

Do they provoke your frustration when they line up in

orbit near your

ear,  sounding themselves in the eroding work of sense?


By night the board is crowded like a supercluster.

How deep do the stars go in the sky?  How far beyond the

silent "e" of your tongue, and the long "I" of your eyes?

What happened to the "l" in "world," the "e" in "love"?

Do you make the exceptions in your mind and, from small

nearby wisdom, persist in loving error?

Unbegun

That would be a promise

I could not keep, he thought

when the fuselage opened before him,

to receive your care and fear

and return it with leaping protection,

an assurance before the fact of loss,

for that which is lost is already

beyond the matter of love aforethought.


Clauses inferior to their descendants,

I would have thought there in the darkness

with the droplets floating between

and us reaching out to the screen

as though it held an assuring promise

that we might emerge less and more.

She threw me in,

and her head turned, it seemed, to the floor

with knowledge and bitterness

and a certain drama of nudity.


The only thing that made sense was your

sudden kiss and clasp, and my before-

dying analogy and the true three dimensions

of that in-between—don't let

her run away, she shouldn't be

a runaway. There wasn't enough

darkness though even for us, nor for all the others.

Upward, flew us.

Eric Wertheimer lives in the desert with Mili, Dani, Aya, and Tupac, where he is Professor of English and American Studies at Arizona State University. He is the author of Underwriting: The Poetics of Insurance in America (Stanford University Press, 2006) and Imagined Empires: Incas, Aztecs, and the New World of American Literature, 1771-1876 (Cambridge University Press, 1998). He has published his poems in a variety of journals over the past ten years. His other book projects include: Pretexts: War and Writing in the Early Republic, and Within Trauma: Politics, Poetics, Praxis.

Made in the USA
Monee, IL
07 July 2026